HOW TO PRAY TODAY

Religious Experience Series

Edward J. Malatesta, S.J., General Editor

Volumes in Preparation:

Religious Experience Series

Volume 4

How to Pray Today

by
Yves Raguin, S.J.

Translated by John Beevers

ABBEY PRESS
St. Meinrad, Indiana 47577
1974

How to Pray Today is the English translation of *Prier à l'heure qu'il est*. It is published by contract with the original publisher, Vie Chretienne, Paris, France.

Library of Congress Catalog Card Number: 73-85334
ISBN: 0-87029-028-2
© 1973 by St. Meinrad Archabbey
Printed in the U.S.A.

Contents

Introduction

How to Pray Today: the title of this book is both a question and an answer. It is not a discussion of the difficulties of praying under today's actual conditions, but an attempt to give a real answer to the needs of so many people who no longer know how to pray.

The traditional forms of prayer, particularly of personal prayer, are regarded as so out of date that one no longer dare mention them to the faithful. One can speak freely only about communal prayer, yet the forms this prayer takes have, for many people, turned the green pasture of Christian prayer into a desert. A new formalism is well on its way to rob Christians of the freedom it claimed it was giving them.

Now if there is one sphere in which warmth and spontaneity must never be stifled it is certainly that of prayer, for prayer is the expression of my relationship to God. This relationship must declare itself in all my life, for each fibre of my being is linked to God. My prayer must embrace every kind of human activity. It is a constant and many-blossomed flowering, springing from my being a child of God within that unity in which all men are brothers.

Prayer blossoms when we turn to Him who is the source of our being and the final goal of our existence. Whether alone or with others, we grasp at this relationship and express it by a simple thought, a hymn of praise, a plea, a cry of distress, an offering of some kind, a helping hand given to someone, joining with other people in a religious ceremony or making a humble personal gesture.

Each time I wait for, long for or meet this Being who is my God, I am at prayer. I think that the very word "prayer" ex-

1

presses all this, for it comes from the Latin word "precare" which means "to supplicate." So I think that prayer can be defined as the attitude of a man aware of his frailty before the Most High. Even to be aware of the distance which separates us, of the great gulf between us and Him, is a supplication in itself, that of a helpless creature, who longs, through the grace of Christ, to have the quality of life transformed.

Just to present myself before God is a cry for help and a prayer, for when I realize my insignificance I am driven to ask to experience in all its full and over-flowing richness that Life which has been offered me.

But it is not only the asking for something which is prayer. My whole nature, the moment it realizes how dependent it is, cries out to be something more, seeks even to become like God.

Such is the prayer of my inmost being, the most basic prayer I can utter, for it is a cry from the essence of my humanity. It expresses itself through all the thousand and one human activities, through the most sophisticated to the simplest. I disown none of them, for my prayer is not limited to any particular aspect of my life. The Church which wants to be the church of the poor cannot reject the prayer of the poor, that simple prayer so despised by the intellectuals.

If one lives in a country where popular devotion is expressed in offerings, in bodily prostrations and in incantations, one comes to understand the importance of these forms of prayer which are both individual and communal. We must not make the mistake of many priests who pay a brief visit to such a country. They are full of new ideas and want to cleanse Christian worship of every practice they consider superstitious or a relic of the past. But if they enter a temple and see people praying with endless obeisances amidst clouds of incense, they are deeply moved and never think that what impresses them there is what they condemn among Christians.

I know that every age has its own tendencies, but, whilst making what adjustments are necessary to accommodate those of the present day, it must not be forgotten that these contemporary tendencies are reactions against what was done in the past, and that reactions of this kind tend to distort what is right and proper. The pages which follow will try to keep open a door for those new tendencies without, as far as prayer is concerned, sacrificing any human needs, whether they are those of the poor or of the rich, of the intellectual or of the simple soul who goes through life asking no questions.

Chang-hua (Taiwan)
October 26, 1969

Part One

Prayer and Faith

1. *Because I Believe*

As prayer is the expression of my relationship with God, I can pray only if I believe in this relationship. Now this is what Christ came to explain to us. He came to tell us once again that we have a Father who loves us and wants to have a close friendship with us. Under the gaze of the Apostles, Christ made manifest His link with His Father in His words, His manner and His deeds. And it is on them that our own prayers must be modelled. As He lived out this relationship with His Father in front of the Apostles, He also made them aware of that hidden world to which He bore witness. He awoke their faith.

To anyone who has faith, prayer presents no problems, for he knows he comes from God and that he owes gratitude and homage to the Author of his being. He is well aware that God is so great and so different from him that he cannot lay hold on Him or understand Him, and his prayers become a humble acceptance of His mystery. But when the revelation of Christ strikes home and he realizes that this God, however incomprehensible He is, does reveal Himself in His Son, he ventures to believe that through this Son, the Word of God, he can grasp something of the divine mystery. As he advances along the path of prayer, he comes to recognize that between him and the world of God there is developing a much stronger and a much closer bond than can ever exist in human relationships. His prayers bring him into union with God. He experiences something new which, until then, he could believe in only by faith.

As he continues this advance, his relationship with God becomes easier and more natural, for man's capacity to understand and to love gradually develops and, at last, perfects itself. Yet prayer always remains the humble entreaty of a being longing to be given more light and more love. Man can never storm the Kingdom of God. Lucifer knows what the attempt cost him. On his journey towards eternity, man must keep on praying and he will find that God's greatness grows as he finds out more about Him.

Prayer always stays linked to the world of faith and seeks always to draw nearer to it and finally to dwell within it. If we shut ourselves out of this world there can, of course, be no relationship between us and it. The worldly world limits its interest to the goals which human society can achieve, and in this world men concern themselves with their careers. Their supplications are for material favors and their prayers are nothing but requests to an organization or a government. The only time they are reminded of what prayer should be is when they implore a friend for help in times of need and distress. Then it is: "I beg you, I beseech you," but there will be no one to whom they can appeal when they realize that the whole fabric of their life is shattered and they are reeling to destruction.

They still pray during periods of ordinary unhappiness, but they neither know how to nor, indeed, are able to when they experience profound suffering. They are well aware that no other human being can accompany them into their own personal abyss. That is when faith is needed, but they no longer have it. If they cry, like Jonah from the depths, they are certain there is no one to hear their entreaties. So they are silent. They suffer without hope, for they have relied on themselves and on their fellow humans. But what can our fellows do when the very roots of our being are torn with agony and the foundations of our lives are crumbling? We must not be gulled by any trust in the soothing idea of society coming to our help. We shall be abandoned when our sufferings are at their greatest.

But to the man of faith, this is the moment when God responds. He alone hears the prayer which rises from the pit of human desolation.

* * *

2. *Firm in Faith*

The feeling of being heard can produce faith. Take someone who knows the teachings of Christianity and who greatly admires Christ and yet cannot be a Christian because he cannot accept that Jesus is the Son of God. To him, Christ is merely a man. He recognizes the unusual qualities of this man, but—to him—they do not mean that He has any special divine origin. In such a case, his recognition that Jesus is someone extraordinary has nothing to do with faith.

But it might happen that this man is involved in a personal crisis and then just says: "Lord, if You are what You claim to be, help me!" It is then that light may flood in upon him and he will recognize that Christ is more than a man. He has found faith and discovered that another world exists and that its laws are revealed by Christ. Another universe in which he did not want to believe has been opened to him by prayer.

Prayer must be based on a faith born like this or on one which develops naturally out of a Christian upbringing.

In the Gospels, Our Lord repeatedly praises the faith of those who ask Him to heal them. They pray to Him because they believe He can heal them. Without this belief, they would only marvel at the astonishing things He said. He performs no miracles for nonbelievers, for those miracles which He does do are the disclosure of a power which must be recognized by faith. In Nazareth, He commented on a passage from Isaiah to stir the faith of his listeners, but they would not go with Him into the realm of God where He wished to lead them. These Nazarene folk never thought for one minute of asking miracles from their famous fellow-citizen and were quite indifferent to the faith He offered them. They believed they already had it.

The first kind of prayer we must use, or rather the essential attitude to adopt before we pray, is to place ourselves with confidence and with no reservations before Jesus. This is not always easy. So we must be like Mary, who listened to Jesus sitting at His feet, like Martha who listened as she was bustling about preparing a meal, like the woman taken in adultery awaiting the word of forgiveness from Christ, like Peter who, despite his hot blood, was quietly attentive to his interior promptings, like John who watched, listened and eagerly took everything in, like Joseph who said nothing but knew that he was wholly involved in a mysterious affair in which God needed his participation even though he could not grasp its full significance, and like Mary who kept hidden in her heart all the disclosures about this mystery in which she was the prime agent.

They all show the same, tranquil, unwavering commitment to the mystery revealed by Christ. What is very striking is the intensely aware attitude of the Blessed Virgin when the angel spoke to her, of Elizabeth when Mary visited her, and of John the Baptist when he met Christ. It is the same with John and Andrew when they spent their first day in the company of Jesus, and with the crowds who heard Him speak.

We must be like them if we want to advance in the way of prayer. We must be eager to catch any hint about the nature of the divine mystery which springs from a text, from a passing thought, or from a moment of spiritual illumination. We must let our minds dwell on them and keep coming back to them. What starts to strengthen and deepen our faith may be something quite small—a phrase in the Gospels, a spiritual impulse, a touch of grace, an act of charity to a poor fellow-creature, or the sharing of a neighbor's burden. What it is is not very important in itself, but what is important is that it enables us to know God a little better and we must let the light it throws on Him fill our minds for as long as possible. At first our prayers were superficial, but now they grow more and more earnest and our entire being must be involved in prayer.

Thoughts sparked off in the way I have just mentioned can nourish our souls, for days, weeks and months. The faith they stimulate can become the great reality of our existence. All our spiritual life can revolve around the knowledge that God loves us. We no longer need to be convinced by intellectual arguments, for we believe the words of Christ in the Gospels. And we must make sure that this belief affects the whole tenor of our thoughts and strengthens our faith.

To make sure we stick fast to the truth we have glimpsed, we should do well to rivet it to our souls by seizing on a phrase which sums it up: "God is love, if you only knew what God is offering." These words have a luminous power which becomes more evident the more we meditate on them with faith.

* * *

3. *Intelligence and Faith*

Many people are prevented from advancing towards a greater knowledge of the secrets of God because they will not adopt the spiritual attitude which faith demands.

For example, there are the two commandments about loving God and loving our neighbor. To understand the first of these necessitates our pondering over it in the light of faith, for the nature of this love is beyond the grasp of human intelligence. To meditate on it with faith means that we must accept all that Christ told us about God and His love. The basis of all thought and of all prayer about this commandment has been given us by Christ. Many Christians feel they are walking along a rocky path when they try to love God, for He does not have for them the solid reality which they would know if they accepted the gift of faith offered them by Christ, and which was lived out by Him during his own life here. For many the stressing of the second commandment is really a flight from faith. They try to justify themselves by quieting the words of Christ and St. John on the love of one's neighbor being a sign of loving God, but they forget that for St. John, St. Paul, or for Christ Himself there is never any doubt that loving God comes before anything. It is obvious that this insistence on our relationship with our fellows is a roundabout way of rejecting that relationship with God which cannot be experienced without faith. As they do not wish openly to reject this relationship, they turn to that other commandment which everyday experience lets them understand without any need of faith.

In fact, Christ wants to make us realize that there is only one commandment: to love as God loves. As we are human, our love goes out to our neighbors and to God, swinging, as it were, between two poles. But when we meditate on love we can do so using merely human standards and so we have no need of faith. Yet when we try to understand love in relation to God we have to do so in the light of faith, for God is known to us here by what Christ has told us about Him. I can understand something of the love God has for me and the love that I should have for Him by what I know of a husband's love for his wife, and of the love between parents and children. All I know of the love that springs from obeying the second commandment throws light on the first. When I pray, this experience of human love gives me some understanding of the love of God and even a real flavor of it.

But if I do not go beyond this in my efforts to understand what the love of God truly is, I am living in a world of self-deception and, unless I change my approach, I am mistaken if I think that I love God. Our Lord says, in words of unmistakeable clarity: "Anyone who prefers father or mother to me is not worthy of me. Anyone who prefers son or daughter to me is not worthy of me."

It has been claimed that this means only that Christ is to be loved with more warmth and intensity than we give our relatives, but in reality His words indicate a wholly different scale of values, for whoever deserts his parents for Christ loves them more than ever. He surrenders himself to another love which, though it is just as much "love" as that he has renounced, is yet on an entirely different plane.

Comparison of this love to human love will have been useful to us, but now, once and for all, we must stop comparing the two if we are to grasp what this new order of love is which we are invited to join. We must change our way of thought. So far, we have tried to understand by drawing on our experience. Now this experience must be ignored.

We must say: "Lord, You have said to me: 'God has so loved the world that He gave His only-begotten Son.' There is nothing in my experience which can make me understand such a love. You say: 'As the Father has loved me, so I have also loved you.' How can I realize the Father's love for You and how much You love me?"

These revelations made to us by Christ are heavy with mystery. That is why we must study them with faith and wait for the Holy Spirit to give us understanding of the words of Christ. We shall make manifest our longing for this understanding by our attitude of docility, by our eagerness to learn and by our humble waiting to be enlightened by faith. If we pray with faith, we shall say continually: "O Lord, I believe in Your love, but I cannot understand what it is." Prayer must go beyond the strivings of the mind if it is to develop in faith and by the promptings of the Holy Spirit, whose purpose it is to fill our waiting emptiness to overflowing.

* * *

4. *Silence and Faith*

Silence is the manifestation of our need to be quiet so that we can rediscover calm and peace.

In this silence we withdraw into our inner being and so become more able to cope with business worries, the row our children make and the trouble they cause us. Everyone longs for silence as he longs for rest or sleep.

A Christian appreciates it at two levels: the usual one, that of every man, but he also recognizes in this silence the world of faith. On the first level he can rediscover himself; on the second, silence allows him to give his undivided attention to the mystery of God.

We should practice this prayer of silence throughout our life. It offers itself to us the moment we come up against a mystery which is beyond our ordinary human intelligence. Silence is the first step towards spiritual rapture, and this rapture or ecstasy is the product of faith working in the depth of our being. We begin to learn what faith means to do for us the moment we turn away from ourselves and keep silent before God.

Silence is the beginning of ecstasy. We are silent not because of the pleasure it gives us, but because we know that the truth which fills our soul cannot be grasped by our natural intellectual faculties. Many people are checked in their search for God because they continue to pray in what I call a natural manner. They wrestle as best they can with the truths of religion, trying to understand them by reason and by comparing them with their human experience. They feel that if they let up in their prayers for a single moment they will lose all the benefits of the time they have spent in meditation.

This activity can give them great knowledge of the Gospel,

and its mysteries, and such knowledge can give them a certain satisfaction if it is enriched by their sensibility and their intelligence. But it will never have true spiritual depth. Their link with the world of faith will be built merely on theories. Faith will not be given the opportunity of bringing to life all the knowledge they have gained by their spiritual reading, by their meditation and contemplation and by their deeds.

Faith cannot become a living reality within us unless we meditate, contemplate and act within a framework of faith. Faith is offered to us by Christ and we acquire it only by placing ourselves before Him in silence. We must be docile before God in order to receive His teaching.

If we do manage to grasp a little of the mystery of faith, a vast, unknown territory stretches out before us. When a child learning to read comes across a sentence he cannot understand, he repeats the words, looks up from his book and waits for them to be explained. The mysteries of the supernatural will not be revealed to us by words dropping down from Heaven, but faith will gradually give us understanding. It may come from the text on which we are meditating or rise from the depths of our intelligence when it is illumined by faith. But it will take time, a lot of time, and that is why we must continue to use this prayer of silence, praying and waiting and open to receive the light that will surely come.

When I write of silence, I do not mean ordinary silence, but one which is charged with longing and expectation. The Liturgy is full of this silence, especially during the season of Advent. It is a silence which discloses an inner emptiness which we long for God to fill. It is a void which cries out for the light of His presence.

No matter what passage from the Gospels nor what spiritual truths we meditate upon, we must grow accustomed to creating a great, silent void within ourselves which awaits the coming of God. Let us take these words, for example: "Before Abraham was, I was" and pray over them in this empty silence. To compare them with "I Am who I Am" opens up infinite vistas before us. What more can we do? Shall we go on to think about the omnipotence of God? That will serve for a time, but what must be done is to pray over these words in silence, that silence which means we are waiting expectantly for God to make us understand in the depths of our soul who He really is. Gently, very gently our souls will be flooded with the light of faith in which we shall see a little way into the mystery of God.

All men need periods of solitude and silence, but nowadays we seem to be afraid of them. We can no longer live alone and so we find it hard to pray in solitude. So why do we not go into a church for a few minutes? Let the housewife put down her shopping basket and the businessman his briefcase and immerse themselves in silence. If we do that we shall strengthen our ties with those we love and also with those strangers going about their affairs in the street outside, all unaware that a brief silence says more than words can utter.

* * *

5. *Humility in Prayer*

We cannot batter our way into this realm of faith. If God does not respond to our plea, we shall never cross its threshold. This is why Christ says: "I bless you, Father, Lord of heaven and of earth, for hiding these things from the learned and the clever and revealing them to mere children."

Many rebel against the necessity of having to beg for divine illumination. It offends their human dignity. But where does man come from and what is the source of his greatness? I am well aware that God has given the human soul great power and astonishing grandeur. When we pray, it often happens that we feel a great surge within us of love and creative force—an experience which makes us fully aware of our worth. This inner power which intensifies all our human abilities also sweeps us nearer to the divine.

It is then, at the moment when we are at our peak, that we may become aware in the background of the power of the Almighty. If we do indeed see the divine power revealed in this exaltation of ourselves, we shall not find it hard to say: "O Lord, my God, all this strength comes from You, yet no matter how great it is, it is not enough to enable me to comprehend You, and I ignore all it offers me so that I can listen to the revelation of Yourself which You have given me in Your Son."

The Scriptures are full of such avowals by the Psalmist and the prophets. They knew that no man, by his own power, can enter into the secret places of God. They pray with great humility and simplicity: "Hear my voice, as I cry to you for help. I cry to you, Yahweh, my rock! Do not be deaf to me."

As long as we are content merely to brood over spiritual ideas and writings, we shall never realize how impossible it is by such means to enter into and fathom the mysteries of God. But all will change the moment we are ready to place ourselves before Him in a silent appeal for faith. We can do nothing but beseech God to look upon us and answer our plea. Only a second or two before we do this we can still be puffed up with pride in ourselves, but, at this moment of appeal, we find that, before the holiness of God, we are but sinners and we see, too, that all our learning is but ignorance.

In all our prayers we must ask God to give us understanding. We can always grasp the literal meaning of words, but it is another matter to understand them as Christ wishes us to understand. In Christ, the printed words become spiritually alive.

Even if we do manage to grasp some part of the meaning of what we read, we have to admit that it has a deeper significance which will be revealed to us only after our friendship with God has deepened. The knowledge of God which has been promised us is without limits. So we must never abandon the humility with which we pray; indeed it must deepen as we draw closer to God.

We should not mistake the nature of this humility. It does not spring from a timorous, morbid feeling of guilt, but is the simple awareness of the infinite distance which separates us from God, even though He offers us that intimacy we ourselves would offer to a most cherished friend. It is the humility of a free man who knows his freedom is made complete when he acknowledges his dependence on God.

If we meditate on the Trinity, we can get some enlightenment from all that the Fathers of the Church have written and, intellectually and spiritually, we shall be able to grasp enough to let us savor something of the mystery of the Trinity, but it will never cease to be a mystery, and there will come a moment

when we have to say: "O Lord, what must I do to understand
more?" The reply will be: "Have done with trying to understand and listen humbly and submissively to the promptings of
the Holy Spirit." If we meekly recognize our helplessness, we
prepare ourselves to receive the light God will throw on His
mysteries.

What is this light? It is the spiritual warmth with which the
Holy Spirit infuses our knowledge and gives it life. Phrases
gain new depth and affect us quite differently. We become receptive and no longer try to give them the meaning *we* think
they should have.

To be humble is nothing more than to see clearly what our
position is in relation to God. It is not enough to recognize this
in theory. We must act according to it and see that our prayers
reflect it. It must be our unvarying attitude and then the divine
light will shine upon us as it always shines in the souls of all
those who are meek and humble.

*   *   *

6. *The Language of Faith*

When Christ came to tell us about God, He used human
language. It could not be otherwise, but to anyone who gives
himself to the study of these mysteries this presents the problem
of the language of faith. A nonbeliever can interpret this
language in a wholly human way, and it then means nothing
more than if it were ordinary speech. It gives no clue to any
understanding of the mysteries.

Now the words of Jesus are intended to convey something
quite different from their conventional meaning. The unity of
Christ's teachings can only be appreciated by going beyond
their obvious, everyday significance. The unbeliever has to
deny the honesty of Our Lord and refuse to believe the truth of
His words, for he could explain them only if he accepted a
state of things in which he does not believe.

When Christ begins to speak of His Father, it soon becomes
clear that He is not referring to Joseph. Here we have the first
problem. When He explains that this Father is His Father in
heaven, he presents us with a new problem by revealing a rela-

tionship which is beyond our grasp. And when He declares that His Father and He are one, he shatters all human definitions of the relationship of father and son. This assertion of His is the starting point for considering the mystery of the Trinity.

No one feels any uncertainty about the literal meaning of Christ's words. He uses no obscure philosophical terms nor is His style at all involved. This is why His revelation of the divine mysteries comes across so strongly. Christ wishes to awaken His disciples to a reality they never suspected. This awakening develops slowly and it is the very ordinariness of the language in which the revelation is couched which makes them recognize the supernatural truths.

Many refuse to follow Jesus on the way He wishes to lead us. Was it not because He declared that He was the Son of God in a unique sense that He was condemned to death? Those who would not accept the truth He revealed understood perfectly the meaning of His words, but they refused to let themselves be swept into the kingdom which had been opened to them. But when a Christian prays, he listens to the language of faith and follows Christ to enter into the Kingdom of God.

A life of prayer and meditation will enable us to give the language of faith the same meaning that it has for Christ, but yet it must be recognized that we shall never be able to grasp the full meaning of this language. Christ alone possesses its total sense, and it is by the Holy Spirit that He discloses it to us.

What is the unity Christ speaks of when He says that His Father and He are one? We can understand the plain, grammatical meaning of His words, but what we have to understand is the way of life of the divine Persons, the whole mystery of the begetting of the Son. To understand the unity of the Father and the Son is to comprehend them both in their very being and to grasp the harmony of their existence. Language about them will become meaningful when we ourselves share in the intimate life of God, but this we can do only in Christ Himself. Now, if we wish to follow Christ, He has laid down very stringent conditions. We must keep His commandments if we want to have the certain knowledge of His divine Sonship. We must carry our cross with Him if we want to know Him.

"My teaching is not for myself: it comes from the one who sent me; and if anyone is prepared to do His will, he will know whether my teaching is from God."

Accordingly, to be able to understand the words of faith demands a total commitment of ourselves to follow Christ. For the purpose of these words is to make us discover the existence of that divine life which—working in us—we call the supernatural life. It is by being willing to live this life in Christ that we render ourselves able to recognize the divine life in ourselves and in God. It is a simple process. We trust Christ and listen to all He tells us of the divine secrets. We obey all His commandments and do all that He wishes us to do. Because of our docility, both He and His father love us. "If anyone loves me he will keep my word, and my Father will love him, and we shall come to him and make our home with him." This is how God manifests Himself to those who love Him. The Father and the Son will send the Holy Spirit.

They who would like to penetrate the mystery of Christ's words without living with Christ will never be able to do so. As we pray, we know that His words are Spirit and Life. His language is the Word of God, and to listen to this language with faith is to be alert to Life.

*   *   *

7. *Attentive to the Divine Life*

In the spiritual life it is supremely important to concentrate on the enigma of our relationship with God. This relationship is essentially what God has told us of His life in and through His Son. The life of prayer of a Christian must revolve around this central point. Every kind of our activities as human beings can be a prayer, and all of them can grow and develop in the light of faith. To want to limit the expression of our attentiveness to the divine mystery to communal and liturgical prayer is as absurd as refusing to recognize private and personal prayer. Our devotion to the divine life must be the coming to full flower of all our human activities beneath the sun of faith. In that solitude which makes us fully aware of ourselves, we catch a glimpse of our beginning and our end. We recognize that God is the ultimate explanation of our fleeting existence.

In our life among our fellows, we want to share the life of that community which Christ came to establish among those who believe in Him. Holy Communion is a banquet where all become aware of a new unity among the Christian family. We are no longer alone and it is as a chorus that we invoke the coming of the Lord. At this banquet, the Christian waits, attentive in faith, for the sign from Him who has already been, who now comes and who will continue to come.

Waiting upon the mystery of faith, the whole human situation is pregnant with Him who comes. Attention is the sign of hope. The final words of the Apocalypse express this waiting: "The Spirit and the Bride say 'Come.' Let everyone who listens answer 'Come.' Then let all who are thirsty come: all who want it may have the water of life and have it free." And: "I shall indeed be with you soon. Amen; come, Lord Jesus!"

These are the words which end the Bible. They voice the expectation of the whole Church until the end of time. Longing, expectation and hope for this water of life spring up throughout our human life, but the water will flow to waste in the sand if we are not there to catch it and guide it to the trees whose sap it will become.

We must become accustomed as we pray to stay alert for indications of that divine life which is hidden from us. To watch out for them is well on the way to intercept the outpouring of this life and let it flood into our minds and souls. That is all that God expects from us: a humble attention to the mysterious things he accomplishes in the universe and in human souls. We scarcely ever look beyond outward appearances and never perceive the vast, active working beneath them. By faith we know that God alone gives meaning to the world and to the whole of our existence. Every action of ours has infinite reverberations both in this world and still more in the spiritual world.

Each one of us is linked to God by a spiritual bond, but this relation acquired a new dimension when Christ came. "Think of the love that the Father has lavished on us by letting us be called God's children; and that is what we are." All creation is the daughter of God. Every man is the son of God, but in Christ this title has a new meaning.

As we pray we must get accustomed to fixing our attention on these mysteries which are exclusive to Christianity in such a way that we cling to them by an act of faith.

What produces this new relationship? We cannot know but we can believe in it and give all our attention to what we believe. This is not a piece of vain imagining, for we do not invent the object of our attention. We wish to fix our gaze upon it so that our spiritual life connects up with the reality of the divine life whose existence Christ came to reveal.

This attention we must give to the heavenly mysteries will last until the day when we shall discover and understand them in the light which streams from God. Our prayer is a waiting in faith which we must maintain until the day of vision comes. It sometimes happens that a sudden new perception will illuminate the darkness. It will give our eager waiting a still greater intensity, for what is shown to us is but a trifle compared with what is still to be discovered: "We are already the children of God but what we are to be in the future has not yet been revealed; all we know is that when it is revealed we shall be like Him because we shall see Him as He really is."

In waiting, we must in all our prayers and in all our acts be quietly attentive to that which is outside us and beyond us, for it is that which gives meaning to everything.

* * *

8. *The Experience of Faith*

In faith we enjoy a certainty which bypasses our human intelligence, for it is wholly based on the experience and testimony of someone else. In prayer, no matter what method we use, we try to experience this world of faith. It is a legitimate effort for, even though the object of faith is beyond our reach, we get in touch with it by human language and experience.

We try to understand what faith offers us with our intelligence and to feel it with our heart and soul. It is the whole of our life which is involved in getting to grips with this spiritual world which we want to know as well as we know the world in which we live. It is certain that our good human qualities are going to give strength and reality to our faith. If we delight in beauty it will be easier for us to enter and live within the mys-

teries offered us by faith. Every aspiration we have towards all
that is right, beautiful, great and holy prepares us for the experience of faith.

It happens sometimes that, after a long, dusty spiritual journey, a truth disclosed by faith suddenly takes on a personal
meaning. It drives deeply into us and links up with the most
profound of our human experiences. We then really know and
feel this particular truth which has hitherto been only a simple
belief engendered by faith. Our human nature realizes a truth
which is beyond human knowledge.

The danger is that we shall hide this truth away in our feelings or thoughts. This, unfortunately, happens too often, and
what we relish then is no longer a divine truth or the presence
of God, but only a memory which we have trimmed down to fit
within our human capacity. We have hugged to ourselves what
God offered us as if it were something of our own. This is no
longer prayer but self-love.

There is only one remedy: we must cease enjoying this
memory and plunge again into faith seeking what neither our
intelligence nor sensibility can offer. If we are to experience
faith we must always be detached from what we know through
our senses for, although the experience is a human one, it yet
goes beyond our simple capacities.

The profound emotion which communal prayer can arouse
brings us close to God, lifting us like a great ocean swell. At
its most profound, this experience produces an intimate union
with God which is both personal and communal. But seizing
hold of God at the height of this emotion is like every other
human clutching at Him: it is the ecstasy in face of the divine
which we feel as human being beings which allows us to know
that other ecstasy demanded by faith.

One can say that love is the blossoming of faith. Faith gives
way to love as we advance into the intimacy of the mysteries of
God. A human being who loves—if his love is warm-hearted
and not egotistical—will be marvelously well prepared to make
the passage from faith to love. To love and to know that one
is loved makes one expand and open oneself to divine love.
Two beings who love each other with a pure love and seek to
know God are going to find this love gives them wings to fly
to Him. Divine love will appear to them like a new blossoming

of their human love. They will see no difference between them. This is true, but here again must be repeated what has been said about all spiritual advances on the human plane. The experience of human love must end in rapture when confronted by another love which plunges its own roots deep within the roots of this first love, yet soars so high that, to realize it in its fullness, the human love must be purified and sometimes even sacrificed. Ultimately it is the divine light which must transform our humanity and lead it to its complete fulfillment.

Such is Christian prayer. It teaches us to discover the world Christ has revealed to us and to live in it as naturallly as we live in the world of men. We have to enter it to see, to grasp and to savor what Christ proposes and reveals. This divine world will become more real to us than this globe on which we live. We have discovered divine life in us and we seek to live it in all its fullness, integrating it into our human experience. In this life of prayer we are docile before the Son of the Father: "No one has ever seen God; it is the only Son, who is nearest to the Father's heart, who has made Him known." We pray to know in the light of the Holy Spirit, the Son and the Father who has sent Him.

*   *   *

Part Two

The Method of Prayer

9. *Time for Prayer*

At the present time it seems difficult to convince good Christians, even monks, nuns and priests, that a time should be put aside for prayer. I know very well that even the expression "to put aside a time for prayer" causes a violent reaction in those who think there is no longer any need for prayer. If the important thing is to give our time to the service of others and consecrate it to human relationships, it no longer seems very clear why a time must be reserved for converse with God. The idea of a direct relationship with God has lost any meaning for many people. Relationship with God is now achieved through a relationship with our fellow-humans. Now if we wish our prayer to blossom into a constant alertness to the mysteries of God, it is difficult to imagine how this can happen if we do not wish to consecrate a little time to it. Some people will be able to give each day some time—short or long—to prayer. Others will be able to pray only occasionally in the evening or in the morning, or on a journey or during work which does not occupy the whole of their mind. God's love is always present, yet our regard for it is normally vague and diffuse. Now what is important is that it should become the object of our total attention if only for a few minutes each day.

It is true that the relationship to Christ and to God which holds the first place in the Gospels and the Epistles does not, in itself, demand time. It demands the involvement of our whole being. But, as human beings, we cannot be aware of this demand and obey it without giving it the attention which takes up time. The difficulty is that the fixing of our attention on the invisible is a burden which can be borne only by faith. The Church knows this very well, which is why she has instituted times of prayer which are periods in which we regard the divine mysteries hidden in the fabric of the universe. It is for this reason that she has put apart the day of the Lord with its ritual and its prayers.

In Christ and through His eyes, the Church contemplates these mysteries and she invites the faithful to do the same. She tries to make them recognize in this dedicated time somewhere outside time where God is. The "seeing" Church invites us to become attentive at a time and a place which become the bases from which to contemplate the invisible and the eternal. This time, cut out of our ordinary life, gives notice of that which lies beyond time and space.

The Church demands that priests and religious shall give still more time to waiting on God, for this is their function in the Church. If they refused to make this gift of time they would betray their vocation. To offer time is to offer oneself. When we give our time we give our attention, our presence and all we can give. We are there for another. When we pray we are there for God, for a God who is there for us.

This business of the gift of time is at the very root of human relations. Is a young man who wants to win the love of a girl going to say: "You know I love you, but I haven't any time to spare for you"? And what would a wife think if her husband could not afford her a little time when he gets back from work? The gift of time is the gift of oneself.

I realize that we object to devoting any time to our relationship with God because we cannot see Him. Christ, though, has told us enough of this relationship to enable us to enter into it. He was well aware that the Apostles found difficulty in praying to their heavenly Father, for He was a Father never seen by man. But to reassure them and give them a starting-point, He told them: "Who sees Me, sees the Father."

Christ Himself, Son of God though He was, gave time to personal prayer as the Gospels mention several times. We know He spent many hours and sometimes whole nights in prayer. It has been thought that He prayed only to set us an example, but I think that, as He was a man, He had to spend time in prayer. This time was essential for the awareness of His relation to God to come to fruition within Him as a man. The relation with God He enjoys throughout eternity had also to be realized during the years He lived as a man.

The amount of time to be given to prayer is usually settled by the Church—for all the faithful, for priests and for all in religious orders. But it is fair and sensible to allow a certain freedom. The essential thing is that we should decide to consecrate to God a period of prayer which matches our personal needs. Those who want to pray at the behest of an inner impulse wish for no rules. But such freedom would be unsuitable for others, and they should submit to a strict regimen. For them, discipline will be a great help, for, contrary to popular belief, regular practices bring freedom with them.

When we have reached a state of constant union with God, time takes on a new meaning. A fraction of a second may give us a glimpse of infinity, and a thought which flashes through our mind may, through faith, grant us entrance to all God's secrets. By faith, time is transformed into eternity and our human nature takes on something of the divine. Such is the value of time for those who wish to find God.

*   *   *

10. *Prayer Together and Alone*

These two kinds of prayer go back to the beginnings of Christianity. Our Lord told his disciples that, when they wanted to pray, they should go apart into a room to be alone there with their Heavenly Father. He also said that when several are gathered together in His name, He is in the midst of them.

But nowadays it is fashionable to disparage personal prayer as if it could only be the product of egotism and of a desire to escape from the demands made on us by loving our neighbors. A retort to this could be that many who pray together are seeking a sense of human togetherness rather than Our Lord.

The argument can go on endlessly, but all experience shows that, in the end, the major events in the life of the spirit occur when we stand alone before God. Today we are very inclined to think that salvation is not a personal affair. But the Gospels tells us continually that it is the individual who must render an account of himself before God. And who will be there then to speak up for him? "Of two men in the fields one is taken, one left; of two women at the millstone grinding, one is taken, one left." This is the great truth of human life: we live together in communities, but God picks us one by one and, in the end, each one of us is responsible for himself before God.

I know that he who prays alone is not necessarily nearer to God than he who worships at Mass on Sundays. But yet those who sing in the Sunday crowd and relish being amidst their brothers and sisters in Christ may perhaps only be the dead members of a Church which lives despite their death.

There are Christians who think they come much closer to God by praying alone, but in fact they cannot rise above the self-satisfaction they feel at believing this. Indeed, this solitary prayer never lifts them above a weak sentimentality and, having turned Christ almost into one of themselves, they no longer feel anything but a vague love for Him and an equally vague hope of attaining Him. On the other hand, this private prayer has nothing about it of that heady emotion stirred up by group prayer. But both kinds of prayer can lead us astray. Yet both can be perfect prayers.

We are going to our final destiny as a people, the people of God, as a chosen body, as a flock led by Christ, our Shepherd. We go forward as the Church of Christ and this Church will not disintegrate on the death of its members. We form a body, the Mystical Body of Christ. So it is in common that we praise Christ, that we seek Him and that we receive Him. In the heavenly Jerusalem it is still together that we shall sing to Him who has redeemed us.

For this vast community of the redeemed, the Church has formulated a liturgy and a cycle of prayers which express her faith in Christ and the worship we should offer Him. When we join in this worship, we really live with the Church, all of us praying with one voice and heart. Such prayer and such worship can exist only if, like all liturgies, it is formal enough to suit all times and all places. Such a liturgy is essential to express the universality of the Faith. The collective thrill which runs through it is always controlled and, even though it touches our human nerves, it goes far beyond naked emotionalism.

This form of prayer engages in its rhythm all the strength of feeling that man wishes to involve in his relation to God. This is why there must be prayer within more restrained groups, prayer which will allow the intellectual aspirations of its members to manifest themselves more freely. This is a need which is not satisfied in some churches which are too traditional, and this has caused the spread of what one might call "underground" churches. The Christians who attend them are looking for what they consider a more genuine form of prayer and they are drawn together by the similarity of their mind and character. It must be recognized, though, that this communal prayer of isolated groups risks making impossible participation both in the worship which is always essential to the Universal Church and also in all personal prayer.

These two types of communal prayer must not make us forget that our personal relationship with God remains all-important. If it is not constantly cultivated, something is missing from the spiritual personality of the Christian. The great mystics have always ascended the mountain of God alone.

*   *   *

11. *Learning to Pray*

A thousand methods of prayer have been formulated and there are attempts to teach an art of prayer. But prayer will never let itself be hemmed in by any particular method. It escapes all bonds the moment it becomes true prayer.

If prayer is the expression of our relationship with God, it can be defined on the level of what we do and say or, more accurately, on the level of that attitude of spirit, individual to each one of us, in which and by which we express our relationship to God.

The difficulty is that we cannot manage to utter our inmost feelings without also making use of gestures, acts, rituals and words. So that is why there is an art of prayer which can be taught, and if we use it we shall become aware of what is the right interior prayer for us and it will grow and flower.

One day the Apostles said to Jesus: "Lord, teach us to

pray," and Jesus taught them the Our Father. In giving them this formula for prayer He did, at the same time, reveal to them the reality of God as Father, taught them to praise Him, to long for His coming and to ask for the necessities of life.

Henceforth, the Apostles knew how to pray, and since then the Our Father has been said untold millions of times in every language of the globe. It is *the* prayer of Christians, the prayer which meets the needs of many, for it is the prayer Our Lord taught His disciples.

But there are some who still ask: "What are we to say when we want to pray, for we find it hard to pray without using words?" To answer their question we must return to the treasury of the Church's prayers. It is vast and has accumulated throughout the ages. The Psalms and the prayers of the prophets hold a privileged position in it. Millions of Christians have read and sung their words to replenish constantly their awareness of the divine Presence in the world and, borne by faith, to help them to leap towards Him. They are words rich with centuries of belief and with the passion of a mystical fervor. "In your loving kindness, answer me, Yahweh, in your great tenderness turn to me." Millions have prayed thus, gazing beyond this world to the Kingdom of God.

To learn to pray, it is enough to return to these texts, to read and reread them and accompany their thought as it moves continually from our world to God's. To savor a text of the Psalms is already to savor the reality to which it awakens us: "God, you are my God, I am seeking you. My soul is thirsting for you." We can learn to pray by going again and again to these texts and letting the image of God which emerges from them grow slowly within us.

But it may happen that these texts lose their power and that even the Gospels become insipid. Everything which has so far sustained our prayers loses all meaning. When a soul reaches this state, it again begins to beg and plead to be taught how to pray: "I thought I knew how to pray, but I realize that all I do leads me nowhere."

This soul is looking for a way of prayer without the aid of texts and words. It believes it is in that spiritual state called tepidity. Nothing of the kind. It has simply reached that stage in its spiritual growth where all language seems pointless compared with the reality towards which it beckons. Words have lost their meaning. It wishes to grasp directly and immediately the relationship which has been forged by prayer between it and God.

What must this soul be told? To be still, to accept the silence of all human language so that it can be attentive to another language. This is to have learned to pray with faith. If I ask God to help me, that presumes that I believe in His power to intervene in the affairs of this world. If I praise God, that means that I believe my homage reaches Him in His glory. If I stay in silence before Him, plunged in adoration, it is because I believe He is my God. When I am flooded by a profound awareness of the divine Presence, I can understand it only by an act of faith.

Finally, what we have to learn if we want to pray is that we must move continually from the world in which we live into that world of faith which Christ came to reveal to us. Once we have grasped what prayer is, we can use any method just as a musician, able to play several instruments, picks up the one that pleases him at a moment of inspiration. Many people are musical, and there are people who understand prayer but have never learned any method. On the other hand, just as some can play an instrument without being musical, there are those who utter prayers and yet do not truly pray. But they can learn: both the spirit of prayer and the many ways of expressing it.

*   *   *

12. *Methods of Prayer*

All methods of prayer are to be valued according to their effect on our attitude to God. We can study them just as we learn to play an instrument, but we must distinguish between an elementary exercise and one which is inspired.

There are simple methods and some are so sophisticated that they are quite beyond the reach of the ordinary faithful. Experience alone will tell us which method suits us best. Some are better fitted for the needs of monks and nuns than for those of the laity, but every Christian should be free to use the methods recognized by the Church and sometimes those of non-Christian religions.

In studying ways of prayer, we must not be deceived. There is not one of them which gives us access to God Himself. What they can do is to create in us a climate in which faith can expand and one which will render us receptive to divine action.

If we do not spend a fixed time in prayer, the question of a method hardly crops up. Many Christians pray briefly each morning and evening by reading a few prayers or a passage from Scripture. During the day they may pause for a moment to ask God for forgiveness and help.

But when a regular period of time is set aside for prayer, the question of methods does arise, for prayer then becomes an exercise which we seek to perform as perfectly as possible. The usual method suggested is that known as meditations. This means taking a text from Scripture dealing with a sacred mystery and examining it word by word with our mind and heart fully engaged. This analysis is made to reveal its full spiritual implications from which we can draw guidance for our personal life. This exercise is done in the presence of God. It is not a piece of mere literary or exegetical analysis, but a reflection on a mystery of faith which will establish it more firmly in our mind and soul.

What we should expect to get from such meditation is a growth of faith and a much clearer insight into the particular divine mystery presented in the text. But it is hard to estimate the extent of this deepening of faith, and the factors by which we judge if our mediation has been successful will often have nothing to do with the real business in hand. We may, for example, ask ourselves if we have increased our understanding of the text we have been studying and whether or not we have suffered from distractions.

Too often we shall say: "I meditate badly"; "I felt like dropping off to sleep"; "I could not concentrate at all." But these things are something quite apart from the really important matter, which is to have shown a fundamental docility before God.

There are very elaborate methods of concentration which produce a profound tranquillity. With discipline and determination, we can reach a state of perfect repose beyond all perception and all thought. The soul is static within an all-pervading peace. Is this a state of prayer? It depends on the interior disposition of the person who has reached that state. If he is enjoying a profound peace which is only the feeling of complete unity within himself or with the world, there is, properly speaking, nothing truly religious about it. But if this peace brings a sharper perception of faith and an opening of the spirit to the divine world it is prayer.

In any case, there is no need to consider any particular method of prayer as essential. We can use one, but should feel free to change it. The trouble is that to help those who meditate to use their time of meditation fruitfully, they are put into a straitjacket of methods of prayer which it would be better for them to abandon, or at least be free to use or reject. One comes across monks and nuns who have scruples about praying as they wish because they have been conditioned to certain methods.

Basically, every method is a form of coercion which aims to help us to concentrate our attention on God. This does not come naturally to us, for the truths of faith are not innate. So these methods compel us to keep our attention fixed on matters beyond what we can see and know naturally. If someone adopts a method he is like a farmer who digs a well to get water for his fields. He does not dig at random first in one spot and then another. He chooses a place where he thinks there is water and gets to work, digging steadily. He is delighted when he gets down to damp earth and overjoyed when he reaches the hidden spring. The water gushes up and irrigates his land. All he has to do then is to take care that his well neither silts up nor falls in. He who seeks God digs thus, using the means which suit him best.

*　*　*

13. *The Prayer of the Rich and of the Poor*

The prayer of the rich is the prayer of those who have studied a great deal and are able to cope with more elaborate methods. The prayer of the poor is that of the vast majority of people whether they are Christians or not. The prayer of the rich is that of intellectuals who take good care to have nothing to do with a simple piety they consider unworthy of their learning. But the poor fall back on whatever is at hand to support their prayers. They look for a symbol which will let them express their faith and need no subtle methods. Very simple formulas enable them to express their faith: the Rosary repeated over and over again will nourish their faith until they die, and the Rosary culminates each week at the Sunday Mass.

There are always pious snobs who have nothing but contempt for the devoutness of the poor. It was the same in China where official Confucianism utterly despised popular piety. The Christian Church, thank God, has never done that. But the danger of this is always present, for many mistake intellectuality for spirituality.

The piety of the masses needs to be simplified and purified for, left to itself, there is a risk of its sinking into superstition. Yet we must not forget that the majority of Christians are always made up of these poor and they need a form of prayer adapted to their human needs and one which will help them to go to God in their own way. Words, however splendid they are, pass over the heads of nearly all the faithful unless they are rephrased into sentences they understand and are used to.

In the liturgy, rich and poor meet on the same level at that moment of silence when the mystery is expressed in such simple terms that the distinction between rich and poor ceases to exist: "This is my body and this is my blood." He who is greatly learned cannot enter into the knowledge of the mystery except by faith. And it is perhaps here that the poor man, unhampered by too much thought, goes ahead of him into the ecstatic realization of the divine presence.

"Our Father in Heaven" . . . this is no moment for the learned to indulge in involved speculations. Along with the poor he says "Our Father" and this Father—who sees all hearts—is not concerned with the sublimity of our thoughts.

What is extraordinary in the development of the spiritual life is that whoever enters it rich with knowledge and learning gradually loses all regard for them as he discovers the way of faith. He learns that neither the sublimity of his thoughts nor —even less—the subtlety of his methods of prayer give him access to God. As the intensity of the divine light increases, he sees the uselessness of all his learning, and he also discovers that his virtues are nothing and can buy no favor from God.

His learning is like a stream which vanishes the moment it enters the immensity of the divine ocean. A simple glance replaces long and complex theorizing. In his prayers he relies on a phrase, a word, a thought. He entered the world of faith like a Pharisee, a virtuous Pharisee, and has gradually withdrawn to the far end of the sanctuary. He finds himself poor among the poor of God. He can no longer count on his righteousness and beats his breast. To call on God he no longer knows what to say but "God," "the Lord Jesus Christ." That is all that remains of his great learning. But in this poverty he discovers the infinite richness that God offers him through faith. A stream of joy and knowledge flows over him.

At the same time, the poor fellow who knows only the *Our Father* and the *Hail Mary* prays as best he can at Mass and keeps quiet when he cannot understand, and yet, without knowing how, he slowly discovers the vast treasures within the mystery of God. He has entered God's house through the door which is always open to the humble. His wondering gaze, illumined by his faith in God, has discovered the existence of things he never suspected existed.

How do these poor of the Kingdom of God know so many things and understand them so well? Simply because they always remain docile before the Holy Spirit. They have never had anything of which they could be proud. They have resigned themselves to being what they are and God has showered them with favors.

There is no opposition between these two types of people if they journey on to the end, for then there is neither rich nor poor. The light of God searches the heart and not the appearance. However rich we are in learning, we are always poor before God, and this poverty is our glory if we agree to accept the wealth He offers us.

* * *

14. *A World without God*

Mystics experience the dark night of the soul and feel abandoned by God. Their prayer is barren in a universe from which God has withdrawn. In their writings we have the echoes of

their distress as they seek the Lord. Many today feel that God
has withdrawn from the world. He has hidden Himself and left
it to its own devices. It is useless to seek Him in the distant
regions of Heaven, for there no longer is a Heaven. It seems,
indeed, that there is no longer any place at all for Him in a
world which grows more and more self-sufficient. How can we
pray to Him and ask Him to intervene in the world, since we
can no longer see how He could?

We are all afflicted by the situation in which God has put
the universe. It is now hardly possible to ask people to see
God present and active in all things, for they are too afraid to
create God in their own image. They say that God is only the
energy working in the inmost recesses of men and matter. In
face of such an attitude, how can we rediscover the meaning
of prayer?

In fact, the state of the world has not really changed. If
science hopes that one day it will be able to explain everything,
man will still not be able to understand himself, for to do that
he will have to get outside himself. Yet he could understand
himself if he would trust the words of someone who was a man
yet came amongst us from outside the world. If His revelation
is accepted, it means that the essential factor to make prayer
possible has been inserted into our outlook, and for the man
who believes and realizes from whence he comes his first act
will be one of profound adoration before Him who is the source
of everything.

If we think for a moment about the advance of science, we
notice that the more it discovers the further away do its hori-
zons retreat and the problems facing it become not merely large
but immeasurably huge. And there seems no reason why this
process should suddenly reverse itself so that one day the
source of all life becomes subject to our control. Man could
accomplish this—on one condition: if he could become that
unique and omnipresent Spirit who has created everything.

When we are faced with what we cannot understand, our
humility is a prayer, for we fall into a state of rapt wonder
when we are confronted with the unknowable. Even if we
hesitate to give it a name or regard it as a person, we should
be able to rediscover in the modern world that attitude which
human beings have always had when faced with the mystery

of their beginning and their end. To explore the world of the atom or to walk on the moon only lessens any hope that we shall one day reach the limits of the universe.

For the believing Christian, everything is much simpler. He knows that God is the Father of all things and that everything has been created by the power of His Word and quickened by the Holy Spirit. But, along with those who do not believe, we can simply carry on living in that state of excitement to which we are driven even by the progress of human science or we can look at everything with the profound admiration of a child who senses mystery. And it is from this that is fashioned the prayer of the man who is aware of the greatness of "what is" or "who is" the source of everything.

We can also begin the examination in depth of ourselves, although in spite of all the efforts of psychologists and psychoanalysts the human personality remains as mysterious as ever. Why a man behaves in a certain manner can be explained. But who is going to tell me where I have come from and why I am what I am? Man cannot explain himself. However deeply I plunge within my personality, I shall always come face to face with something beyond myself which sets up responsive vibrations in me, and yet is something which I can neither investigate nor understand. It is this which throws us into a state of rapture before that which our intellect cannot grasp and which is quite outside ourselves, before that Other from whom we realize we have our being.

A nonbeliever will see this Other as the basic natural principle underlying all things. But, because of Christ and what He revealed, we know it as a person and call it Father, the Father of all creation. We call the relationship between us the Spirit of Love.

Why not try to develop the readiness to pray by using what we can understand of the enigma of ourselves together with a simple acknowledgement of our link with God? When we become aware of our relationship with God, let this awareness flower as a prayer. When we feel the power of love in our flesh, in our heart and in our mind, why not let this feeling fulfill itself in prayer to the Father of all life and of all love? When we enjoy a human love let us deepen it by thinking of that infinite love which quickens every other kind of love.

And so prayer will be the springing into bloom of the whole of our life and thought. Our life will again have meaning because of values which are just as up-to-date as they were when the world was young.

* * *

15. *Prayer without God*

As I said at the start of the last chapter, humanity is beginning to experience the absence of God or, at least, that is what some people wish us to feel when they proclaim that God is dead. God is not dead to millions of people, but to millions of others he has vanished over the horizon. Christians are affected by this and, if they are to continue to believe, they must clarify their idea of God. It is perfectly right and proper to do this, but it is a process which does make prayer more difficult.

If we have been able up to now to pray easily and feel God very near to us, we should not cling to our memories of this, but continue to contemplate in silence, though it will seem an empty exercise and one which brings no response. But it is the only way of purifying the idea of God we have built up in our minds. We must cling fast by faith to what Our Lord came to announce.

When God draws near and discloses Himself to us, He very quickly withdraws to prevent us from creating a false image of Himself. We must accept this and not bemoan the loss of the transports we have known. They were only a stage on the journey which we had to reach and pass. Although we may feel He is absent, God is still with us. We gain knowledge of Him through His absence, for after He has given us some inkling of what He is, He at once wishes to make us realize that He is quite beyond our full comprehension.

This is a basic truth for anyone who seeks to find God by prayer. There is no need to be distressed when God seems to desert us. If we accept the mystery of His absence, we shall draw near the enigma of His nature. Abundance and dearth succeed each other on the journey towards God. It is the great truth of Christian life.

Everyone who has even a little experience of prayer will admit this, but will still ask what to do when God has gone away. We must resign ourselves to this vacuum and not try to fill it by creating a personality out of our imagination. This is what many do, or are tempted to do because they cannot endure the feeling of helplessness.

The best thing to do is to focus our regard on this inexpressible mystery and make this concentration the very core of our prayer. Let us wait tranquilly in the darkness. To do this we must have faith.

It is also beneficial to pick up our Bible and read again some of the words that have particularly struck us. As we come to them afresh, we shall find that they seem to have lost their meaning. This does not mean we have lost our faith, but that a new insight is stirring within us and making us realize that we have so far tasted only the husk of the real meaning of these passages. If it seems that the Gospels have lost their meaning, it is because God is preparing to make us understand them far more fully.

If anyone has this experience in his own prayers, he will not be troubled by what is happening in the Church, for with Vatican II the Church has entered into a dark night of the soul. The problems facing her are as fundamental as those with which the great heresies of the past confronted her. She is asking in what sense she must understand her own infallibility and the primacy of her popes, how she should expound the Scriptures and what is the significance of her own tradition.

The Church must do what the mystics do in times of spiritual crisis. The apparent silence of God must become the very basis of her prayer. She knows she has the guidance of the Holy Spirit to the end of time, but how will it operate? She is in great distress, for she knows very well that her integrity is not just a matter of remaining faithful to the past. She no longer knows how to explain what she is and also sometimes what she believes. She shows her faithfulness by being completely docile in the Holy Spirit. But what is the guidance of the Holy Spirit?

If we look beyond her institutional formality, we find that she waits humbly upon God as she studies the Gospel bequeathed to her by Christ. She also asks, like our mystics: "Have I really, up to now, fully understood everything?"

The whole Church utters this humble prayer. This is why, in this spiritual darkness, some have dreams and others visions.

Some believe they are inspired by the Holy Spirit and talk nonsense. Others are truly inspired, but they find it difficult to get a hearing. Some search silently for the truth; others wrangle. But, as yet, no one can see very clearly. But why should we panic?

The whole Church must be willing to enter into the night-enshrouded desert. The mystics teach us that it is then that God becomes most active deep within our souls. As we pray in this darkness, God is getting ready to flood us with light.

*   *   *

16. *The Sacramental Presence and Prayer*

In recent years, Christian spirituality has changed. There has been a great effort to do away with certain pious practices in order to focus Christian devotion on the Eucharist and the preaching of the Gospel.

The offering of the Holy Sacrifice has become a more communal affair to the extent that for some what is important is not so much the Sacrament as the prayers of the congregation. The Christian no longer feels, as he once did, that he is under the influence of a Sacrament which is complete in itself. He wants to take an ever increasing part in it, and from this it follows that there are people who think that it is only the faith of the assembled worshippers which create the Sacrament and produces the presence of Christ.

This is to forget that it is not any small group which makes the Sacrament. It is the whole Church which perpetuates Christ's sacrifice by the ministry of him to whom she has given this power. During Mass, Christ becomes present by the word of him who is His priest in the Church and is acting on behalf of the Church. It does not matter how many people are there. Christ can become present only in and for the entire Church. This is why the bread and the wine remain Our Lord when the faithful have gone home. The spot where He is present is not limited to a little village church nor to a Eucharistic Congress. It embraces the entire world.

What happens when the priest utters the words of consecration? Who can say? Who can claim that he grasps the reality of what happens when these words are spoken? We can only hold fast to the words of Christ: "This is my body, this is my blood." In the context of the Gospels, especially in the teaching on the bread of life, there can be no doubt about the meaning of these words. In the bread, He gives Himself and the wine is His Blood. I can cling to this and leave the rest to the theologians, aware that they cannot see any more clearly than I until I am called to see the living God face to face, and be filled with His glory.

In genuine prayer, this presence of Christ is an irreplaceable support. We can imagine how the divine presence fills the universe, can see the universe being formed by the divine will, and can be aware of God's presence in our souls. Yet we know that the signs of this presence are not always easy to recognize and that we can easily be deluded.

But this sacramental presence is something quite different. It is offered to me by Him who is the perfect image of God. By the eucharistic rite and His coming He gives us both a sign and a meeting place, the reality of which are guaranteed by Him who is truth itself. It was He Himself who gave the Eucharist to His friends after inviting them to His table. He wanted it to be the total gift of Himself, all that He had been and would be to the end of time.

When He said: "Do this as a memorial of me," he gathered into that moment all the Eucharists that were to come. There are Eucharists at great gatherings, with tiny groups or even without any of the faithful present but, in any circumstance, it is always the complete Christ in the fulness of His divinity and His humanity who comes to us.

This is why the Eucharist of Christ and the Church is the supreme and perfect prayer. All our private and public prayers must be linked with the mystery of the Eucharist. The presence and activity of God in our lives are expressed with the utmost clarity in this act of Christ which is perpetually renewed by the Church. It is the ideal encounter of God with His people in Christ and in the Church. Together they change the bread and wine into Christ: these elements become His body and His blood.

As I have said, this transformation is not dependent on the presence of a few of the faithful, but on the will of the Church exercised by the ministry of the priest. This is why this real Sacramental Presence must remain in the world as the meeting place of God and men. It is the door to the mystery, the silent Presence which speaks through the revelation of the Gospels: "I am the bread of life."

Why not, when you have the opportunity, go into a church and rediscover Him who wishes to be with us? He truly dwells there in the bread which has become food for our souls.

* * *

17. *Constant Prayer*

We must never stop praying. Some of us fret ourselves by trying to repeat prayer after prayer throughout every day. But I do not think this is what Our Lord expects from us in the contemporary world where the tempo of life is so demanding that it leaves us no leisure for thought. Even if we do get a little free time it is taken up by watching television or by social activities.

But there is certainly no general tendency to pray on the hour every hour. This mechanical regularity of prayer has some advantages when it takes place within a fixed pattern of life, but it is not advisable. What is necessary is that, from time to time, we should think of God, and by that I mean that we should see all our daily activities in relation to our life with Him.

Fundamentally our life as a Christian is the same as our life as a human being. Our very existence, all that quickens it and everything that affects us make up the language used by God to reach us. Why then seek Him by other means? Our basic disposition in prayer should be to accept our human condition. Now by doing this we also accept our relationship with God, for the universe and all that happens in it is God speaking to us. But, as we carry on with our ordinary human life, the business of our prayer will be to see, to recognize and to express our essential links with God.

This awareness will always be present in some people. For them the depths of the universe will always open on to Heaven, and what is human is never seen separately from what is divine. They are always in a state of prayer, linking everything to its source and to its final destination. Their prayers take up none of their time, for everything they do is done in a state of prayer. Everything human is always related to God, though it in no way ceases to be human. Far from it. Such people express, by their general attitude, their relationship with God and the rapture it gives them.

If we are to reach this state of being continually at prayer, it is important to gain by faith a vision of the world which embraces its hidden realities. If, during the course of a day, time seems necessary to keep this vision sharp and clear, nothing could be easier, for we need give only a moment—a quick interior act of praise, of adoration or of gratitude—to make very real our immersion in unceasing prayer.

But this kind of prayer remains difficult to achieve, for it counts upon the integration of our world and the world of faith, and that is something which cannot be achieved without a long experience of the depths of the spiritual life.

This is why everyone has to do the best he can to pray constantly. Perhaps the easiest way is for us never to imagine for a moment that we shall be able to find out what we should do by relying only on ourselves. When we cannot decide what to do, when we are worried, when we are anxious about ourselves or others, let us turn to God and ask Him for help and advice. A lot of people can no longer do this because they think God will do nothing and that He intends we should shoulder our own responsibilities without imploring the help of the Holy Spirit.

The ways in which God can help us are mysterious, and even more obscure is the manner in which He can succor those for whom we pray. The difficulty is that we do not know how God can intervene in the events of a world which seems to us to be controlled solely by the will of men. I think we have to believe that creative action did not start and finish when time began; it still continues working in the world through the Holy Spirit. All we see seems as if it can be explained by a kind of determinism, and yet the tremendous mystery which surrounds the universe, and the history of humanity and my own personality remain God's domain, and His power penetrates into the very depths of all created things, into our minds and souls and into the whole of history.

Because of all this, we show by the way we pray the relationship which keeps us close to God, and we believe Christ when He asks us to pray continually.

The prayer of a Christian shocks the nonbeliever who regards the world as self-contained. He thinks of it as something which God has—as it were—flung outside Himself. Yet we should know very well that there is nothing which can exist "outside" Him.

We are not expected to believe that God is going to change the order of history to meet our wishes. There are some things which cannot be done, but there are many others which can be arranged to fall in with our demands, for they coincide with God's plan for the future of the world.

I believe that in this universe of ours we can achieve complete freedom by joining our human desires to the divine will. That is why I still dare to pray . . . and, besides, Christ told me that I should.

* * *

18. *Praying in and through Our Actions*

The question of prayer and action crops up continually. It is thought by many that the two things are contradictory, as prayer is always connected with silence and withdrawal from all worldly activity, and it is true that time given to prayer must be a time of tranquillity. That is why Christ tells us that when we pray we must go to our private room and shut the door. But there are times when prayer cannot be offered in silence and solitude, and then it seems that we can no longer find God in the bustle of the streets and the hurly-burly of everyday life.

As I have said, a period of quiet should be kept for prayer every day, but this period should help us to keep in touch with God throughout the day. We must not think that the union we enjoy with God in solitude is a kind of precious ration which is gradually exhausted by the labors of the day so that, by evening, we have nothing of it left. Our quiet time of prayer should accustom us to find God just as easily in the stir of the world as in tranquillity, in noise as in silence.

Although silence is not essential for prayer, love is, since love is giving all we have to our relationship with God. Now the love that speaks in our innermost being can show itself just as much in our actions. The way we live and work and sacrifice ourselves all show the love which motivates us. Our entire life is linked to God, even in its most urgent secular commitments.

By being willing to act and work in the actual conditions of the human situation we enter into relations with God to co-operate in bringing to pass what He proposes to accomplish in the world. What the human race achieves is the joint work of God and man. God supplies the fundamental and essential power and man works and organizes. No act of ours is creative unless it is done within our relationship with God to further a vast plan which we cannot understand and about which we know only that part which impinges on our own lives. If we link ourselves with God in this joint task, our actions and our entire life are a prayer.

The danger is that we shall lose sight of the greatness of the design and reduce it to purely human dimensions, and so it is essential that we should step back to see matters in per-spective and relate everything to the immensity of the divine plan. Then we shall recognize more clearly how the universe depends on God and that every particle of it is infused with His Spirit. But the Spirit shines forth as much in action as in repose, for God has no perference for either. It is He who determines who shall act and who shall be.

God reveals His presence to him who prays in silence and draws him so deeply into Himself that he becomes comatose and appears to be lifeless. Yet this same presence also mani-fests itself as the life within everything, and another man may find himself gripped and vitalized by this presence and driven to action. God allows us to perform acts which reflect His acts. In them, we share the creative power of God. This God, which perhaps embraced as a Presence a few moments ago, we now embrace as pure action working within the confines of our own activity.

Why do we not humbly try to recognize this active presence of God in the universe and in all our own deeds? Insofar as we have not attained this spiritual insight, and have not grasped the full possibilities of achieving union with the presence through action, our acts will not become a prayer. We should sometimes act and sometimes withdraw into tranquillity, for

we are creatures whose real nature expresses itself in this al-
ternation. But we do well to believe that actions performed
through God, in a state of union with Him, that is, in a state
of perfect prayer, are at one and the same time both complete
rest and full activity. Rest is action and action rest. He who
is lost in God as he prays is working with extraordinary activity in the world. A saint engrossed in the most exuberant
activity always has the core of his being still and tranquil
in God.

This is not too lofty an ideal for those who wish to pray.
Advancing step by step, humble souls can attain it for, from
the very start, Christ and the Holy Spirit will have them in
Their keeping. Less practice is needed than one imagines, but
what is necessary is a lot of love and faith, and the readier one
is to enter upon this great adventure the more of them are
needed.

There are still many things that could be said to explain the
way to pray. But what has been given here will be enough to
enlighten those who seek God. The third section of this work
will extend the boundaries of prayer, but will always bear in
mind that it is the modest, unassuming prayer which brings
understanding of the words of Christ.

* * *

Part Three

The Fullness of Prayer

19. *A World without God Speaks of God*

For anyone who has found God, even the most materialistic world that can be imagined can never be for him a world without God. He finds God even more intimately "mixed-up"—if I may use such a phrase—in the substance and history of such a world. For the saint, someone who understands the innermost structure of created things and their place in the divine plan, a world without God is only something thought up by the human mind, a refusal to accept reality. The world cannot exist without God. What is called the death of God is only an illusion born out of our inability to perceive the reality behind appearances. We have pushed the idea of God outside our human concepts. Yet God dwells in the very heart of the created world. He is the intense life which animates it.

God is not the physical world nor is He the laws which govern it. He is outside them. He is the infinite power which has brought them into being. To become aware of this is to find love, ardor, life and light.

An essential quality of what we call matter is that it can be occupied by the spiritual. Otherwise the world would be inexplicable. The words uttered by Christ when He was in the flesh would be powerless to reveal the Holy Spirit to us, and Christ Himself could not exist. Nor could He have said: "My words are spirit and life." Besides, if this were not so, how could we explain the return of man to the bosom of God, of the creature to its Creator?

What is this mysterious connection between matter and spirit? We must distinguish clearly between them, and yet we know that matter comes from and is maintained by the Almighty Spirit we call God. Creation is an act of God, yet it is an act whose product is distinct from its Creator. It is this distinction which is responsible for the gulf between us and Him and which prevents His creation from revealing Him to us in His fullness.

A man came among us who was God. He was the perfect image of God. Christ offers us in Himself the totality of God, but what this means cannot be properly understood without an act of faith which carries us beyond our natural powers of comprehension. By such an act, we make our own the knowledge the Son has of His Father. It is a knowledge we could not attain by our own natural efforts.

So our knowledge of God can grow and deepen only if we let faith lift us beyond our human perceptions. A human being can thus transcend himself by an act which is yet a purely human act.

What is revealed to us by Christ throws the clearest light we have on the relation of the universe to God. The opening of Genesis gives us a preliminary outline of this mystery, but the Prologue of St. John's Gospel illuminates it:

> In the beginning was the Word:
> the Word was with God
> and the Word was God.
> He was with God in the beginning.
> Through him all things came to be,
> Not one thing had its being but through him.
> all that came to be had life in him
> and that life was the light of men.

It is indeed the very Word of God which is the life of all things and the light of our souls. We are accustomed to differentiate between matter and spirit and sometimes to set them one against the other but, in fact, all life is one within the Word of God. To think of those aspects of the world which seem to separate it most sharply from the spiritual must be at last bring us back to that unique Spirit who has created and sustains all things.

The Master who speaks in the Gospels, whom we call Jesus Christ and who sought to reveal to Nicodemus, to the Samaritan woman and to so many others the source of the living water within them is the same of whom John says: "All that came to be had life in him." Only this conception of the unity of the world enables prayer to embrace the universe. Prayer is the expression of our relationship to God, but this has relevance only when we can rediscover that unity without which no relationship could exist.

Perfect prayer is not content to be a bridge between Heaven and earth: it itself becomes a force and a reality by discovering the origin of all things, the life which is in God and which has been given to men by the Word which creates, illumines and saves.

So my prayer embraces the world and becomes as profound as the life which quickens it. It has no longer any fear of this world from which God is said to be absent, for it finds Him more active there than ever. Nor is it afraid before the divine mysteries, for it sees them revealed in the whole of creation and particularly in Him we call the Word of God and the Image of His Substance.

* * *

20. *The Prayer of Our Humanity*

Prayer must not be something alien to our life. Our human existence must itself be the manner of our prayer.

There is no need for any breach between the world in which we live and the world of prayer. It is true that the time we spend at rest in God allows us throughout the rest of our working days to savor a peace that the world cannot give. To relish this repose and peace is as justifiable as going off to relax away from the noise and bustle of everyday life, to enjoy a pleasant evening with friends, or to spend an occasional morning in bed. The life of the spirit is as much a part of our life as are our other activities, and there must be no feeling of guilt because in prayer we seek to recover the energy we need to make a good job of our work in the world.

What has to be avoided is cutting off our prayer from our life, for that would lead us to regard our existence as a sea of sorrow to be crossed as best we can. Life, with all its joys and sorrows, has been given us to be lived as it is. The whole of it should be the very fabric, basis and content of our prayer. We shall not, after all, be judged on the number of prayers we have added up during our life, but on the way we have lived out our relationship with God. If my prayers are the expression of this relationship, how can it be better shown than in my life itself? I have repeatedly said that, throughout our life, it is vital for us to set apart some time which is totally consecrated to the fullest manifestation of our relationship to God. This must not be forgotten in reading what follows.

My situation as a human being is one of relationship to God, even if it does not seem to me to be as firm and real as that I have with my fellow humans and with the universe in which I find myself. When I begin to find out who I am, I do not know from where I have come, and I have to settle down to live in the midst of what I cannot understand. I discover my mother, my father, my family and the little world in which I grow up. As I realize what I am and when my mother tells me about God, I become aware that I cannot be anything but dependent. But as soon as I accept this situation it does not worry me and I can become fully myself. I experience a kind of dormant ecstasy when I consider all the various elements that have combined to give me life. My acceptance of myself as a human being blossoms into prayer, and this first, almost subconscious ecstasy will, if my interior life develops, become an alert and vibrant rapture as I present myself before God and return to the source of my being.

Buddha saw nothing but suffering in human life, a suffering caused by the transience of all things and by their basic un-reality. For him prayer, if he did pray, was only a request to be allowed to escape this impermanence and unreality. But for the Christian, life is not something from which to flee. It is to be accepted just as it is and with all its pains and pleasures. Christ enjoyed family life and friendship and doing good to others. He lived surrounded by the regard and admiration of the crowds who gathered round Him. He did not reject them, but gave thanks to His Father for the good He was able to do. But He also said that the Son of man had nowhere to lay His head and that all who wished to follow Him must take up their cross.

He faced all human situations and gave meaning to them by relating them to God. It is by this teaching of His that Christianity lives. Every state in which, as human beings, we find ourselves can become a prayer—though not, of course, a state of sin.

If I labor to better society, I may never be able to make it clear that I believe I am trying to make a dwelling-place for God among men. But I know in my heart that this task is the best prayer I can make. I can say, without any lack of reverence, that it is not the holy water sprinkled on it which sanctifies human endeavor, just as it is not the blessing of the wedding bed which makes holy what used to be called "the work of the flesh," but the performance of this act as the children of God should do it. Married couples know very well that the relationship between them is a real one only through the power of their Creator. Thus, the work of the flesh becomes the work of the spirit.

If we pray before the great actions of our life and if the objects we use are blessed, we acknowledge that all things are dependent on God's creative power. True prayer and true blessing become one with our acts and our tools. If we cooperate thus with God and are enlightened by Him, the prayer of our humanity will be able to blossom.

*   *   *

21. *The Prayer of Brotherly Love*

Formerly everybody used to gather together in the church on the market square, for the Christians in the town were identical with the population of the town. Each Sunday, as the names of the dead were read out and the forthcoming marriages announced, all felt themselves part of the great family. Now, in most countries, Christians form only little groups in a great crowd.

But there has developed something new: a feeling of human solidarity among a vast assembly whose members are the children of God. So our prayer must take on new dimensions and become a great brotherly prayer no longer concerned solely with those linked to us by blood or belief, but one which also reaches out to the whole of mankind.

When I pray for those who believe, I am assured that they believe without any doubt that Christ is the unique Savior. But when I look at the vast regions of Asia and Africa and survey the lands of Hinduism, Buddhism and fetishism, my prayer is that their people or their children will one day be able to accept Christ as the light of the world. But I know very well that, at the moment, they are going to God along the path of another faith. I can only say: "Lord, let them find You on the path they travel so that, when the day of enlightenment comes, they will recognize You when they see You face to face."

When I am waiting in airports, people of every color and dressed in every fashion pass through the gates towards their planes. In these airports we see people without really thinking about them. We all know we are travellers—birds of passage. Nothing astonishes us, neither the dress which sweeps the ground nor the most daring miniskirt. Yet this shifting universe of people who think only of where they are going forms a world of neighbors such as one can find nowhere else, for in a few minutes they will all share the same lot and be at the mercy of the aircraft which carries them off.

An airport is not the place for scholarly, contemplative prayers. What is needed is a glance of brotherly love. Such a glance is a prayer, a prayer for the young couple setting off to a new home, for the tourists in their fifties whose children have grown up and gone off on their own and who are now travelling to fill in their empty time, for this mother and her two children who are going to rejoin her husband, for this businessman working away as if he were in his office as he waits for his plane, and for the pilots and hostesses who are making the same journey for the hundredth time.

I don't know a single one of them. I don't know what they need, what their religion is, what their ideals are, what they hope for in their own lives and for those they love. It is impossible for me to take a personal interest in each of them, but if I look at them with the eyes of a brother I am offering them to God so that He can give them His love. My hidden regard for them puts them in touch with God without their realizing it—through the bond of that love which Christ taught us.

Some may be saddened to think that so few among these crowds know Christ. It is true that they do not, yet each of them is trying to live by some ideal, and my prayer of affection for them is not wasted whether or not they are aware of Christ. Anyone who notices a little compassion in someone else is drawn out of himself and can begin to develop. The love God shows to me cannot fail to radiate from me in one way or another, and the whole point of my prayer is to make this love known. The first step is to create a community of brothers among men.

Our mere attitude, the way we listen to people or look at them, even the way we walk can all help to produce this friendly atmosphere and evoke a feeling of security and confidence which helps the traveller to overcome that feeling of melancholy which hangs over all departures. The glance of one who prays is never a empty glance or, if it is, his prayers are not genuine. But what may be interpreted sometimes as a lack of attention is only the effect of being momentarily carried away into the deeps of the spirit. When we awaken from our rapture, our gaze will shine with the light of God.

The world would not seem so empty if there were more people who prayed as they passed along the traffic arteries of the world and amongst the crowds who go to and fro about their business. The presence of God would be more clearly seen. The men and women who do not know the meaning of prayer could at least catch from a glance something other than mere appraisal or lustful desire. They would know that there are people whose role is to act as links between Heaven and earth. Such people are everywhere, in all countries, in all religions, and are both in and outside monasteries and convents. They manifest God's concern for the world and their own loving concern is, in itself, a prayer.

*   *   *

22. *All Men in Christ*

One of the objections made about seeking union with Christ

through personal prayer is that to look for God in this way hinders us from caring for the people who are our brothers and sisters. Such prayer, it is said, can only cut us off from the world and those who are facing its endless problems.

It is true that a certain kind of spiritual exploration some-times produces real egotism just like that of a child who is completely absorbed by the process of discovering himself. One thing is certain: Christianity has never accepted the idea that we should strive only for our own, our individual holiness, that we should try to save ourselves by cutting ourselves off from everyone else and leaving our neighbors, as sinners, to their sorry end. The belief that we should seek only our own per-fection is taught in Buddhism's Little Way—a Way which has made its followers seeks for *nirvana* with no thought for others. In their quest for *nirvana,* athirst with longing for "liberation," they ignore anyone but themselves. They must divest them-selves of everything to reach their goal. They are always soli-tary on their journey and become more and more alone as they advance along it.

In this spiritual progress, the Christian is never alone. He can leave the world and retire to solitude, but he is never alone there. For the purpose of his withdrawal is to meet someone—Christ—and in Him he meets the whole of humanity.

If the Christian withdraws with the purpose of looking only after himself, there is nothing to stop him praying with this in-tention, but what he is doing is trying to monopolize Christ whilst refusing to listen to what He says. The normal attitude of the man who retires to pray is to join in a dialogue with Christ. From the moment he enters into his solitude he is con-fronted with Christ, a Christ who does not want him to turn in upon himself. The teaching of the Gospels is the implac-able enemy of egotism. The man who prays must open his heart to all the world. If he thinks only of himself, the words of Christ will continually disturb his desire to seek nothing but his own perfection.

Christ is not a master who stays close to us in order to teach us how to withdraw into Him. He is the way which leads us into the depth of our being and He is always at the heart of our prayer, yet He compels us to go forward with a warm and open heart and not retire within the shell of ourselves. If we

•

respond, we shall find ourselves closely embracing this Christ who will force us to renounce ourselves.

I know I cannot take Christ to myself as my own personal possession in order to satisfy my egotism. Yet if I can be just a little receptive to His teaching, He will make me see with His eyes and love as He loves. And it is the whole universe He gives me to love. This is what I find in Christ. It is not only the saints who are invited to love the universe when they come to the end of their mystical journey. From his very first step into the solitude he enters to search for God, man finds at the same time the whole of humanity. But it is not an idealized humanity seen through rose-colored spectacles: it is made up of people who need help, of people we dislike, of people who make us lose our temper.

In Christianity, there should not be any self-centered prayers, for God is love and He invites all men to share this love. But there are different vocations in the Church. Some have been called to leave the world and dedicate themselves to contemplating the mysteries of God. It is certainly amongst these that we find the real friends of all the world: people like Father de Foucauld and St. Thérèse of the Child Jesus who discovered that their role in the Church was love.

We do not understand the essence of Christianity if we do not believe in the value of the vision contemplatives acquire in their intimacy with God. Every Christian must be a contemplative, for he is not asked to love only those for whom he has a natural sympathy. He must love all men. But I doubt if merely human virtue will be sufficient for this. I think that, from his contact with Christ, he must have drawn that which makes us love all men as He loves them.

In this meeting with Christ in prayer, I learn that God loves cripples, the maimed and the unlovable. It is through contact with Christ that I shall finally learn to love them too.

*   *   *

23. *Loving My Neighbor*

For many Christians, the discussion in the last chapter seems meaningless. They cannot even imagine how one can seek for God in prayer. They say they can find Him only in and through other people. Others say there is no longer any question of troubling to seek God. Man is the one essential being. Contact with other people is enough in itself. It is unnecessary and futile to try to get in touch with anything outside and beyond this contact. Besides, they say, God gives Himself in man. God is here in man. There is no need to look elsewhere. To pray is to be dissatisfied with our humanity. Does God want this?

Many priests, monks, nuns and lay-people are turned aside from prayer by arguments such as these. They wish to find God only by giving themselves to others and by close association with people. Unfortunately the result of this is often to distort their belief. The Gospels are always being appealed to for support, but they are Gospels from which faith is almost excluded, Gospels so garbled that they become only a useful code for governing human behavior. After a time those who let themselves be carried away by these ideas can no longer see very clearly any part for Christ and His teaching to play. The world has won them over to its opinions.

To claim that the only road along which we must travel to love God must pass through the love we have for our neighbors is to pervert what St. John said in his first Epistle. He said and repeated that if we declare that we love God and yet do not love our neighbors we are liars. We must always come back to God's love for us. But what is true is that it is the love we have for one another which tells us if we love God. By taking an affectionate interest in other people, we shall show if we love God truly, or if our love is only a matter of words.

It is also quite true that God shows His love for us through the whole of creation and especially by this affectionate interest which our neighbors show in us. This is immensely significant for our prayers. And finally: care for others is much more important than being preoccupied with achieving our own perfection. Our union with God cannot be achieved unless those who are nearest to us are especially involved in it. Unless I am strongly linked to other people, unless I am bound to them by common ideals, by affection and by a love which draws me outside myself and makes me unbosom myself to them, I doubt if I can open my heart to the grace of God.

Many so-called mystics suffer because they find no bond

strong enough to draw them out of themselves so that they can live in communion with their neighbors. But faith genuinely held in common opens up the whole world for many people. This is how people vowed to virginity live with the other members of the Mystical Body. They are linked to them by acquaintance, by affection or love, but their hearts remain free from God's unique love. But God's love does nothing to exclude a deep and intimate friendship with someone of the opposite sex. Such a friendship can become so close a union that it will resemble as nearly as is possible in this world that intimacy known in Heaven.

We must not, however, be deceived into thinking that under the guise of a spiritual love we can have the pleasures of physical love. It is true that the experience of spiritual love helps one to find God, but only if it remains perfectly chaste and never has any bodily expression. Otherwise it will end in fantasy and delusion.

How can we know if we are finding God through our encounters with other people and through their affection for us? The only way is to take up the Gospels and reread them with complete honesty and without coloring them with our own ideas and feelings. Then the only question is: What kind of love are Jesus and the Apostle John talking about? Is it the same as that which we are always talking about?

Christ had a group of friends and women were among them. Now Christ remains the pattern of Christian virginity and of all friendships. The whole of His life on earth was made up of meetings, teaching, intimate talks and caring for others. It is by giving Himself to us and by suffering for us that He "meets" His Father again. It is only after having taken us to Himself, mixing with us and making us sharers in His plan of salvation that He returns to His Father's bosom. We must do the same and return to God with, through and by those of our brothers and sisters placed alongside us by God to be, in a very real sense, the means of our salvation.

* * *

24. *The Gospel and Our Prayer*

The goal of prayer is the ultimate union of our life with

Christ's through the action of His grace. This grace is a mysterious gift from God whose existence and operations we know only through Christ. It is only through the faith given us by Christ that we can recognize the final end of prayer and the source of grace. The way and the wherefore of it all is known to us only through the Gospels and the other writings of the New Testament.

Some people seem prepared to say that the Gospel should be rewritten to give Christ a message relevant to our time. They want a gospel which adapts itself to current ideas, accepts them or glides smoothly over them. This is to forget that the men who wrote the New Testament did not have this attitude towards the ideas of their own time. They knew better than anyone that Christ protested against contemporary evils and beliefs. To imagine a gospel which accepts everything in this day and age is merely an idle fancy. Christ came to throw light on the hidden springs of human behavior, not on its externals, and we shall be judged by the standards of a justice concerned only with our interior life and not according to modish catchwords.

The Gospel must not be read in the light of modern principles, but we must judge ourselves by the standards of the Gospel. Actually if we are earnestly seeking the Kingdom of God, there will be little need for judgment for we shall be embraced by the love of Christ.

Our life of prayer leads to our transformation by Christ. How is it done? By the action of grace which works within us when we strive by heart and mind to know Christ.

When I try to understand what Christ is saying in the Sermon on the Mount, I cannot claim to understand at once what He means by the poor, the gentle and the pure. At first I understand these terms only by my own acquired ideas, and yet I know they have a far deeper meaning in the teaching of Christ. What He puts forward as the ideal models are His poverty, His purity of heart and His gentleness.

I have to confess that I cannot attain to these virtues by my own efforts. I try to understand the words of Jesus by the help of others, but, at the same time, I remain humbly attentive to a mysterious action of divine grace in my soul. It is, in fact, this spiritual attentiveness which constitutes my real prayer. I can, if need be, receive great enlightenment from what I know of Christ without relying upon the light of faith. But my really genuine prayer rests in that act of faith which thrusts me into the darkness of God's workings.

Christ has told me: "If anyone loves me he will keep my word, and we shall come to him and make our home with him." And they will send him the Holy Spirit, that Spirit of truth who will "teach him everything." This is what the life of the spirit really means, but we shall not experience it without grace.

In our prayers and actions, we try to behave like Christ as much as we can, imitating Him in His conduct and in the way He relates to His Father. But we know very well that this will be only an outer conformity unless we open our interior life to the work of Christ's grace.

Christ said that the words He spoke to us are spirit and life, and so we must accept the activity of this spirit and life within us. We should never imagine that we have understood the true meaning of Christ's words. It is easy for us to grasp their superficial meaning, but their pith, the essence of Christ, always remains an enigma.

Every word spoken by Christ was said for me and its meaning will not be realized until I have been transformed by it. So the Gospel must be tackled with complete sincerity so that we can be both judged and transformed by it. When we study it and brood over it, we must not be content with its words, but think of Him who spoke them and Who lives now and forever. The Gospel is only a jumping-off point for the discovery of Christ who lived it as He taught it.

I must be guided by the Gospel in every detail of my life and let its teachings illumine my spiritual life. But this is only possible if, with faith, I concentrate all my attention on Christ Himself. That is obvious and it is why the authors of the Gospels wrote them and why they have been followed by so many other writers about the spiritual life.

Christ asks us to come and see. To John and Andrew He said: "Come and see" and they spent the rest of the day with Him. This is how one learns to possess Christ by faith and to be possessed by Him.

*   *   *

25. *The Invisible Face of God*

Our life of prayer will be consummated when we can see the invisible face of God. We cannot see God during our life in the world. But we know that one day "we shall be like Him, because we shall see Him as He really is." By this vision of God, our understanding will be perfected and will pulse with life.

It is toward this that we are heading when we take our first steps along the path of prayer. Then we do not yet know God, but we listen to what His Son tells us about Him. With longing and adoration we take in what He discloses to us of the secret life of God and of the place within it which is offered to us. This other world becomes real to us as we accept it by faith and allow ourselves to be transformed by grace. By this faith, we share the divine mystery. We do two things: we live in it and by it.

As we listen to the words of Christ and see their effect, we try to put a face on this God who cannot have one. The moment we think we glimpse it, it disappears and we begin to look for a more accurate representation of this face which shifts and changes all the time. It is true that by faith we can behold the face of our God, but we cannot put an expression on it.

We are aware that God loves us and that He never turns away from us, and that is why we always stand before the face of God, basking in His love and goodness. Gradually, by prayer, we can become like the Son who never turns away from the face of His Father, for it is this steadfast gaze which makes Him the Son. The face of God appears to us as a presence which forces itself upon us, yet does not hypnotize us. We stay turned toward it because we want to stand before God as His children.

So, although we cannot say what God looks like, we range ourselves before His face so that its light can transform us. We cannot transform ourselves. He alone can do it and does so according to our willingness to dwell in the effulgence of His light. This is the fulfillment of prayer.

To pray is, in the end, to realize that we have to break away from and abandon our roots in this world and leap across to that shore where God dwells.

We delude ourselves if we try to pray without doing this. I know it is very, very pleasant to be conscious of being helped towards God by the combined efforts of those we love. I know their faces help to give a countenance to God. I know we need this help because we are human beings and should not try to be angels. But there comes a time when this human kindness must yield to the warmth of God, and the faces of our friends must fade away lest they mask the face of God.

This must happen sooner or later in the life of everyone who wants to see God. Those we love will stay nearer to us than ever, but their appearance will be transformed as Christ's was after His resurrection. In the light of the glorified Christ, they will seem to us more spiritualized than they have ever been. Moreover, they themselves will, here below, share in that resurrection. They will already be transformed and what they really are will begin to show.

It is in this transformation brought about by the Holy Spirit that the desire of Christ is realized: "That they may be one as we are." This unity is not a matter of natural affinity and feeling, but the work of God Himself.

Our own perfection cannot be separated from that of others any more than it can be from that of Christ. We are unable to save ourselves alone. The Church and all humanity are involved in our efforts, especially those whom God has made our neighbors. But this nearness to us must not become a veil between us and the light streaming from the face of God.

We shall never be able to say: "Oh Lord, I really know Thee.' To the end of time and even when time has ceased to be, we shall always be hurrying in pursuit of the face of God, and it will draw closer and closer to us without our ever being able to say: "Lord, I know You as You know Yourself; I see You as You see Yourself," for God is God and I shall always be the work of His hands.

Such are the prospects shown to us by prayer. They may seem intimidatingly vast and remote, but prayer is not too lofty a mountain for us to scale. All we have to do is to start out to climb it and let ourselves be guided. As we pray, God will come so near that the immensity of the mountain will come to seem nothing more than a grain of sand.

"The Spirit and the Bride say 'Come.' Let everyone who listens answer 'Come.' Then let all who are thirsty come: all who want it may have the water of life and have it free. The one who guarantees these revelations repeats his promise: "I shall indeed be with you soon! Amen; come, Lord Jesus."

*   *   *